Instant Idea Book

Time Saving Tips for Teachers

for Elementary Teachers

- Bright Ideas for Bulletin Boards, Banners and Calendars
  (pages 5 - 18)

- Maximum Mileage from Teaching Materials
  (pages 19 - 40)

- How to Save Time and Work
  (pages 41 - 62)

(includes reproducible pages)

by
Barbara Jean Gruber

illustrations
Ed Salmon

Copyright© 1983 Frank Schaffer Publications, Inc.
All rights reserved - Printed in the U.S.A.
Published by **Frank Schaffer Publications, Inc.**
1028 Via Mirabel, Palos Verdes Estates, California 90274

ISBN #0-86734-047-9

Table of Contents

Bright Ideas for

- ## Bulletin Boards

- ## Banners

- ## Calendars

Add interest, color and pizzazz to your classroom in a jiffy. Decorate plain walls with colorful, fun-to-make projects completed by your students. Best of all, you can use many of these ideas all year long!

FS-8301 Instant Idea Book

Jiffy bulletin board ideas

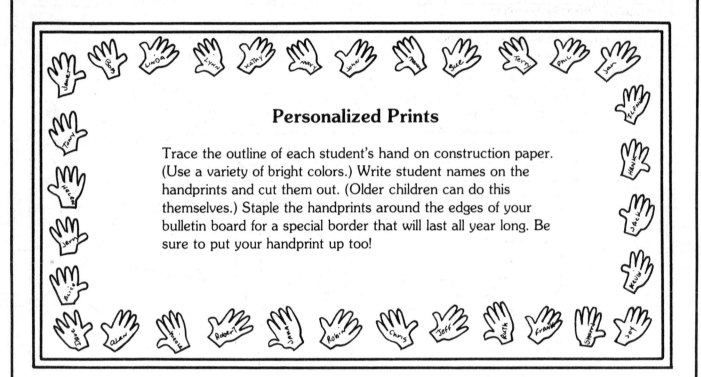

Personalized Prints

Trace the outline of each student's hand on construction paper. (Use a variety of bright colors.) Write student names on the handprints and cut them out. (Older children can do this themselves.) Staple the handprints around the edges of your bulletin board for a special border that will last all year long. Be sure to put your handprint up too!

Letter Locator

Store letters in a shoe box — easy to file and re-use!

Cut letters from both black and white construction paper. (Cut out more vowels than consonants.) Save time by cutting through several sheets of paper at once! Keep copies of each letter in envelopes for easy reference.

Black or white letters look great on most bulletin boards. Be creative — put white letters behind (slightly offset) black ones for accent (or black letters behind white ones).

Batches of Bulletin Backings

Back bulletin boards with your favorite color of construction paper. For a change, put a different color on top. When you are ready to switch back, just remove the top layer.

Use fabric instead of paper. Staple burlap, checked gingham or another plain colored fabric to bulletin boards.

Latex paint stays bright for years! Get official signed permission before painting!

Jiffy bulletin board ideas

Good Work Board

At the end of the week, each student removes his or her work from the Good Work Board. He/she selects a new worksheet, test or art project to put up. The current week's work is taken home on Friday.

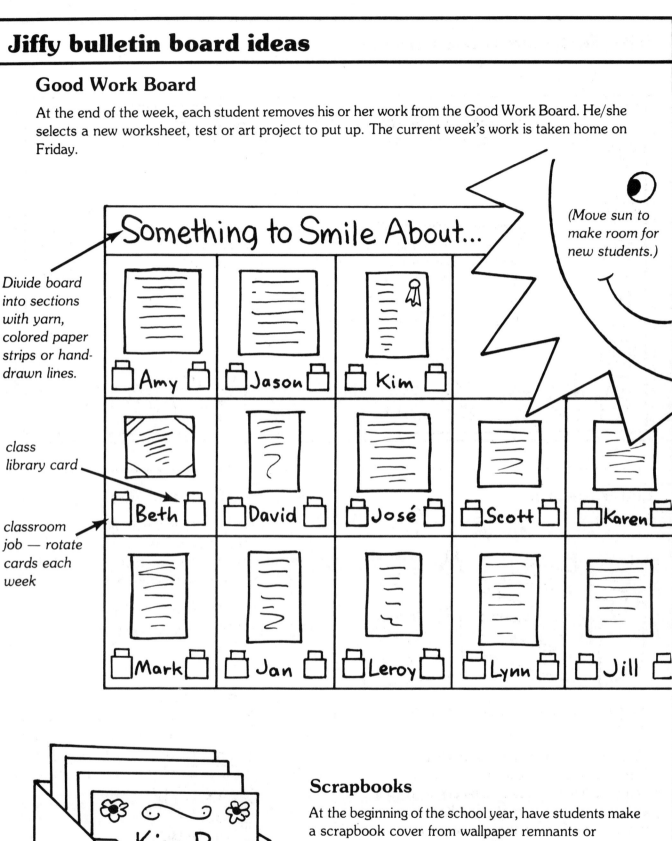

Divide board into sections with yarn, colored paper strips or hand-drawn lines.

class library card

classroom job — rotate cards each week

Something to Smile About...

(Move sun to make room for new students.)

Amy   Jason   Kim

Beth   David   José   Scott   Karen

Mark   Jan   Leroy   Lynn   Jill

Kim P.
Our Scrapbooks

Scrapbooks

At the beginning of the school year, have students make a scrapbook cover from wallpaper remnants or construction paper. When worksheets are removed from the Good Work Board, students paste them in their scrapbooks! The books go home at the end of the school year.

Keep scrapbooks in a box — they get crumpled in desks!

Jiffy bulletin board ideas

Bulletin Boards (above chalkboards)

Today is Monday
May 6, 1983
5/6/83

(chalkboard)

name   extra for
new student

Divide the space on these difficult-to-use bulletin boards to provide a display area for each student in your class. Write each student's name on a piece of construction paper (approximately 1½" x 4"). Staple or pin names along the board so each student has a "spot" above his or her name. Be sure to put up a blank name plate at either end of the bulletin board so you have room for new students. Leave names up all year; simply change seasonal art projects.

Create an information bulletin board — handy for you, students, visitors, substitute.

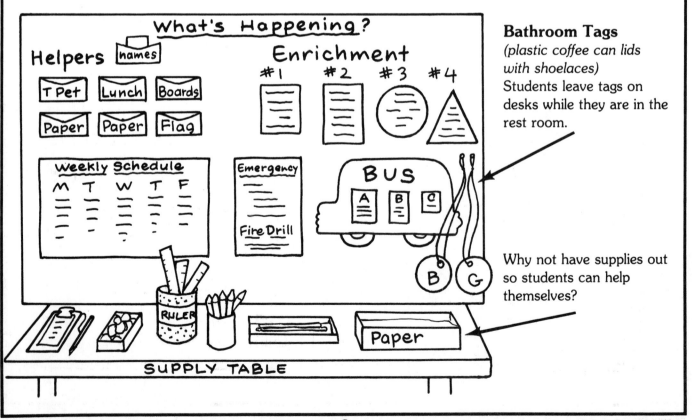

Bathroom Tags
(plastic coffee can lids with shoelaces)
Students leave tags on desks while they are in the rest room.

Why not have supplies out so students can help themselves?

Jiffy bulletin board ideas

Instant Art Gallery

Three strips of heavy paper are all it takes to make an easel for mounting artwork on bulletin boards. Keep easels up and simply change artwork!

Murals—your students do the work!

Staple blue construction paper on the board for sky. Then add green (grass), brown (dirt) or white (snow) paper at the bottom. Write a caption and ask students to make (draw, color, cut out) objects for the mural. Objects are then stapled to the mural scene.

Your wall mural can stay up all year! Just change the theme to coincide with seasons, holidays or social studies and science units.

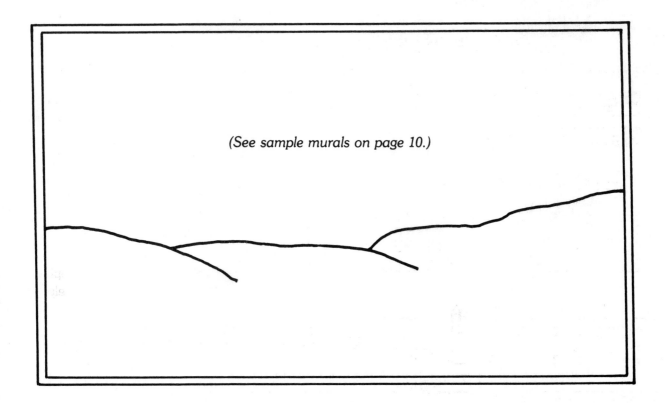

(See sample murals on page 10.)

Jiffy bulletin board ideas

Sample murals:

green "grass" →

It is time for school...

SCHOOL

SCHOOL

To change scene, remove objects and caption.
(Change color of "earth" paper if necessary.)

Underwater world...

brown "dirt" →

Ideas:

green
- fall scene
- spring scene
- summer scene
- farm scene
- dinosaurs

brown
- Indian village
- colonial village
- ocean floor
  (sky becomes water)
- farm scene

white
- winter scene
- Christmas scene
- Eskimo village

Jiffy bulletin board ideas

Instant Graph

This easy-to-make bulletin board helps students read and interpret graphs. Put a graph format on the bulletin board and use it all year long by simply changing the question strip and answer choices. Leave a box containing student name cards near the bulletin board.

Graph Topics:

- pets
- birthdays
- siblings
- states where born
- TV shows
- colors
- games
- sports
- ice cream flavors
- foods
- school subjects

Save to re-use next year!

question strip → **What is your favorite color?**

answer choices

Red	Steve					
Green						
Blue	Laura	Dave				
Yellow						
Orange						
Purple	Mike					

Jill

Names

Box contains name card for each student to use on graph.

Follow-Up Activity

Have students write a paragraph explaining the kinds of information that can be determined from the graph.

For example. . .

Color Graph:
- Most popular color
- Least popular color
- Colors that are equally popular
- Color girls like best
- Color boys like best

Banners add bright spots

All About Me!

An excellent get-acquainted activity for the first day of school! Students fill in information about themselves on the "Getting to know you . . ." banner. Don't forget to include information about yourself!

Use the "Getting to know you. . ." banner for a graph lesson. Individual students or pairs of students choose one topic from the banner for each graph.

Getting to know you...

Name	Birthday	Do at Recess	Hobby	Family	Pets	Favorite Food	Favorite Color	Favorite Subject
Mrs. Gruber	Dec. 30	relax	skiing	1 daughter 3 sons	dog Toto	chocolate ice cream	Blue	Reading
Jason	May 1	Handball	Soccer	1 sister	O	pizza	Red	Math
Mary	Aug 8	Swings	Piano	2 brothers	fish, cat	spaghetti	Yellow	Spelling
Kim	Nov 16	go to library	Read	O	3 cats	Pizza	Blue	Read
John	May 20	play tag	Soccer	4 sisters	2 dogs	taco	purple	Math
Meg	Feb 3	Run	Ski	1 brother	turtle	all ice cream	orange	Recess
Mike	March 19	go to library	read	O	canary	pizza	yellow	Read

Favorite Food Graph - Kim J.

pizza · spaghetti · ice cream · taco · hot dog · hamburger

Give-Away Day

On the last day of school, pick student names randomly and give away the banners. The lucky winners will be delighted to take them home!

WOW! I WON!

FS-8301 Instant Idea Book

Banners add bright spots

No-Sew Paper Patchwork Quilts

Each student makes a 10″ x 10″ square for the paper patchwork quilt. Squares are pasted on a butcher paper background (approximately 3′ x 6′). Squares show up best on dark colors. Quilts can tie in with almost any subject — take a look at this list of ideas!

Topics:
- favorite book or story
- flowers
- birds
- flags
- animals (farm, zoo, woods)
- community helpers
- road signs
- the alphabet
- self-portraits of students
- handprints, footprints
- famous people
- places
- inventions
- holiday symbols

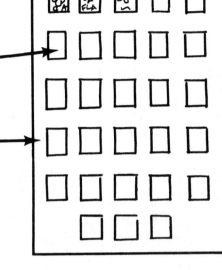

add a caption

square from student

butcher paper

Super-Size Postage Stamps

Make a banner or bulletin board display of commemorative postage stamps designed by your students. Give each student a copy of the reproducible stamp format (page 14). The list of topics above contains excellent ideas for commemorative, super-size postage stamps!

Banners add bright spots

Banner of the Month

At the end of every month, students select work samples to paste on the banner. Hang the banner where everyone can see it — what an easy way to show off the good things that are happening in your classroom!

Space permitting, you can display monthly banners for the entire school year. Parents and other visitors enjoy seeing these colorful displays.

Add your wall calendar, a decorated calendar from a teacher's magazine or simply write the name of the month on the banner.

Short on Space?

When you run out of wall space, offer a banner or paper graph to the library or office to brighten a dull wall. Or, snip the banner apart and give each student his or her part to take home.

Looking for space to post students' work?
Don't forget:
• hallways
• doorways
• sides/backs of cabinets
• sides/backs of bookcases
• "dead" wall space above or below chalkboards

FS-8301 Instant Idea Book

Quickie calendars

Year-Long Calendar

Buy or make a calendar grid to post for the school year. Poke a pin in each date square.

Punch a hole in cute calendar symbols you can buy or make. Hang symbols on the pins for easy removal and re-use.

Your calendar grid stays up all year. Simply change the months and symbols.

Set up a handy shoe box file for calendar numbers, symbols and seasonal pictures. Staple 10 file folders on the sides to form envelopes. Label the folders with the name of each school month. Changing your wall calendar is a snap when materials are organized for quick re-use.

Write-On Weather Calendar

Make 10 calendar grids on butcher paper at the beginning of the school year. Write the name of the month and dates on each calendar grid. Select a student to be calendar monitor for the week. This student draws a symbol on the calendar to indicate weather conditions for each school day.

At the end of the month, paste the weather calendar on your banner of the month (page 15).

Super-Size Write-On Calendar

Make a calendar grid for each school month with large boxes for each date (about five or six inches square). At the end of each school day, write a sentence about the day's activities on the calendar. (In upper grades, a student can be responsible for this.) Post the calendar in the hallway or on a bare spot in your classroom. If you have lots of wall space, save and post calendars all year long. Parents and visitors will enjoy reading these mini-journals of the school year!

Quickie calendars

Calendar Activities

At the beginning of every month, post task cards around your calendar. The activities and tasks should relate to holidays and special events that occur during that month. You can do one or two activities as a group each week, or your calendar activities can be available for students to do during free time!

File the task cards in your "calendar" file for re-use next year!

Make the activities appropriate for your grade level:

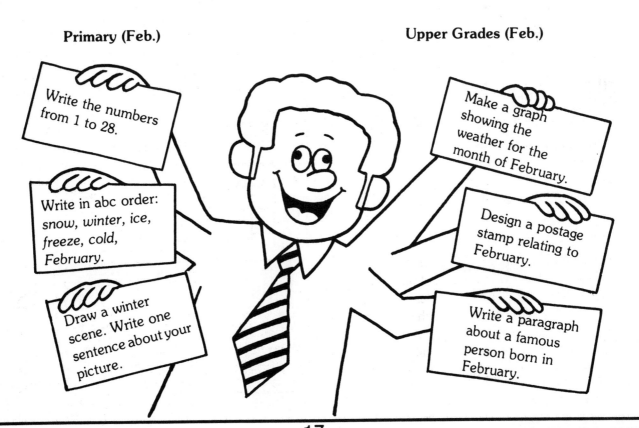

Primary (Feb.)

Write the numbers from 1 to 28.

Write in abc order: snow, winter, ice, freeze, cold, February.

Draw a winter scene. Write one sentence about your picture.

Upper Grades (Feb.)

Make a graph showing the weather for the month of February.

Design a postage stamp relating to February.

Write a paragraph about a famous person born in February.

 **My ideas for bulletin boards, banners & calendars . . .**

FS-8301 Instant Idea Book

Maximum Mileage from Teaching Materials

You'll be surprised by all the terrific things you can do with materials you already have! You don't have to spend after-school hours creating learning activities for students — you have better things to do with your time and energy. Use these ready-to-go ideas that take little or no teacher time!

~uickie Lesson

Short on time? When you need a quick activity, why not cut worksheets into strips? One worksheet can be clipped into three or four shorter activities.

FS-591 Basic Word Skills (2-3)

Place a lesson strip on each desk for students to do upon returning from recess.

✗ Change a Lesson

• Duplicate enough worksheets for each student.

• Cut off and save the written directions before distributing worksheets to the class.

• Read the directions orally, reading two or three directions at a time. Students listen and follow directions until worksheet is completed.

• Distribute the written directions to each student. Students check their papers by reading the written directions and comparing the work on their papers.

(Give to students.)

FS-455 Following Directions (1-3)

(Cut and save. Give a copy to each student to use for checking work.)

FS-8301 Instant Idea Book

Activities for duplicating masters

Mini-storybooks

Don't discard extra copies of reading comprehension worksheets. Save them in a manila folder until you have 8 or 10 different worksheets. Cut off and discard the questions. Staple the stories into a booklet and add a tagboard or construction paper cover. Put the storybook in your classroom library. You now have a book full of short stories with grade-level vocabulary!

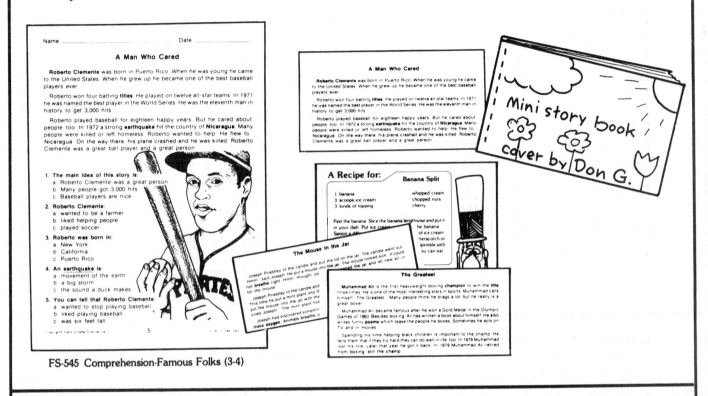

FS-545 Comprehension-Famous Folks (3-4)

Your Signature Please

Save time: Sign award certificates before duplicating them! Just slip the carbon portion from a blank master under each page in your book and sign each award. Make it extra special by using a red or green master!

FS-464 Award Certificates (3-6)

FS-499 Primary Awards (K-3)

FS-8301 Instant Idea Book

Activities for duplicating masters

Play Books

Assemble a collection of plays. Duplicate two or three copies of each play and mount the copies on tagboard or construction paper. (Or, laminate each copy.) Use a three-hole punch and put your plays in a binder. Students can look through the "Play Book" with a partner and select a play to perform for the class. When finished, the copies are returned to the Play Book.

Add plays written by students to your collection!

FS-564 Plays for Kids (2-4)

Sequencing Practice

After completing a sequencing worksheet, students cut the pictures apart and paste them in sequence on a strip of paper.

FS-423 Reading Cartoons (2-4)

Activities for duplicating masters

Desk Top Sequencing

Paste completed sequencing worksheets on tagboard or construction paper for durability. Cut out the pictures and place them in an envelope to create a desk top activity. For self-correction, write a word (one letter per picture) on the reverse side of the pictures. When pictures are in correct sequence, the word is spelled correctly.

reverse side

K   I   T   E

Cut & Paste Matching Games

Make matching games from a book of cut and paste duplicating masters instead of running off worksheets for each child. Duplicate one copy of each worksheet. Paste part of the worksheet on a piece of tagboard or inside a manila folder. Paste each piece on sturdy paper. Keep pieces to be matched in an envelope or plastic bag attached to the matching game.

Reading Cartoons #1
Match the words.

Questions:
1. What is the boy's name?
2. What holds a kite up in the air?
* 3. Would you like to go up in the sky? How? Write a story, or draw a picture.

A 20-page book of duplicating masters makes 20 different activities.

Write #1 on the reverse of each piece. If a piece becomes separated, you can quickly put it back where it belongs!

Tips for using duplicating masters

If print from the back bleeds through while making a photocopy or thermofax master, slip a piece of black construction paper behind the sheet. Now you will get a good copy!

Turn down the pressure on the duplicating machine when using new masters. When masters are producing light copies, increase the pressure.

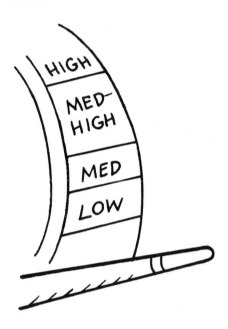

When you need a new copy of a teacher-made duplicating master, run it off on a blank duplicating master. Go over the lines to make your new master. Quicker than tracing over a copy!

See the mouse!

Try spraying the inked side of that almost worn out master **lightly** with hair spray.* It seems to do something magical to the ink so you can squeeze out one more run!

*pump-type or aerosol

Recycling worksheets

After duplicated worksheets are completed and corrected, **save and recycle them!**

Use immediately or set aside to use next week or next month. Pages 25-29 describe 10 different recycling activities, all using a single worksheet.

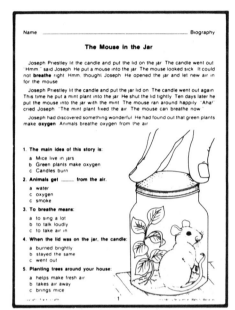

FS-540   Reading Comp.-Bats to Bananas (2-3)

1. Illustrate the story.

Cut off the stories and give one to each student. Students paste their stories on art paper (12" x 18") and draw illustrations. (When you cut off the story, save the illustration or cartoon for idea number 2.)

Recycling worksheets

2. Write about the picture.

Give each student the worksheet illustration that you saved. Students staple or paste the illustration on paper and write a sentence (or several sentences) to describe what is happening.

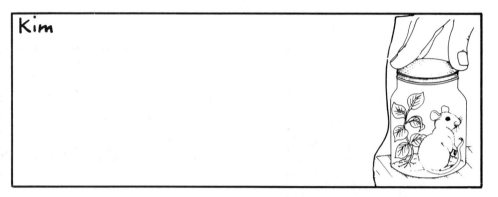

3. Underline statements and write questions.

Students underline three statements in the story, then rewrite each statement as a question on a separate piece of paper. (Or, students can underline three questions and rewrite them as statements.)

4. Alphabetize vocabulary words.

Students circle or underline 10 vocabulary words in the story. They must write these words in alphabetical order on the back of the worksheet or on a separate sheet of paper.

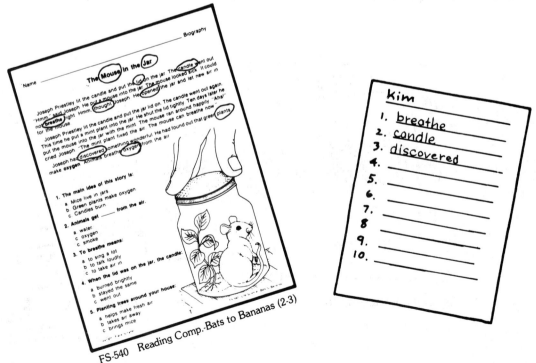

Recycling worksheets

5. Cut and paste sentences.

Give each student a copy of the worksheet story. Tell them to copy their favorite (or the most interesting) sentence from the story on a piece of paper. Then the sentence is cut apart, word by word. Students paste the words in sequence on a piece of 12" x 18" art paper and illustrate their sentences.

Also works with sentences from stories in basal readers.

6. Make posters for vocabulary words.

Tell each student to skim the worksheet story and find a word that is difficult to read or spell. Students will color posters of their chosen words. First, they write or print the word with a heavy black crayon, saying each letter aloud as they print it. Students then add additional bands of color around each letter, saying the letter aloud as the new colors are added. Use the posters to make an attractive bulletin board or staple the posters together in booklet form. Put the booklet in your classroom library.

Works well with words from basal readers or spelling lists too!

Recycling worksheets

7. Create a new title.

Tell students to write a new title for the worksheet story. When you ask students to create a new title, you are asking for the main idea.

Use this idea with basal reader stories too! Main idea is an important skill to practice.

8. Vocabulary expansion.

On the chalkboard, write and number 10 synonyms for words in the worksheet story. Students must locate the words in the story which correspond to the synonyms.

Find words in the story that match these synonyms. Write the number of each synonym above the word in the story.

1. placed
2. fresh
3. discovered
4. joyfully
5. learned
6. marvelous
7. appeared
8. yelled
9. top
10. bottle

Name Kim

The Mouse in the Jar

Joseph Priestley lit the candle and put the lid on the jar. The candle went out. "Hmm," said Joseph. He put a mouse into the jar. The mouse looked sick. It could not **breathe** right. Hmm, thought Joseph. He opened the jar and let new air in for the mouse.

Joseph Priestley lit the candle and put the jar lid on. The candle went out again. This time he put a mint plant into the jar. He shut the lid tightly. Ten days later he put the mouse into the jar with the mint. The mouse ran around happily. "Aha!" cried Joseph. "The mint plant fixed the air. The mouse can breathe now."

Joseph had discovered something wonderful. He had found out that green plants make **oxygen**. Animals breathe oxygen from the air.

Recycling worksheets

9. Students create a worksheet.

Students write three questions about the worksheet story, then exchange papers and answer questions written by another student. Answers should be in complete sentences. Papers are returned for correction to the student who wrote the questions.

Another good activity for basal reader stories!

10. Another student-made worksheet.

Each student writes five statements about the worksheet story, making some true and some false. Students exchange papers and mark each sentence true or false. Papers are corrected by the student who wrote the statements.

Use with basal reader stories too!

Start a file folder of worksheets to be recycled.

Saves time and paper, while reinforcing important skills.

FS-8301 Instant Idea Book

Creating low-cost kits

How to make a kit from a book of duplicating masters:

Duplicate enough copies of each worksheet for everyone in your class. File worksheets in manila folders; store folders in boxes arranged according to skill.

If your kit contains 20 worksheets, number a record sheet from 1 to 20.

Duplicate enough record sheets (p. 31) for each student. Keep record sheets in front of worksheet boxes. (They get lost in desks.) When a student completes page 1, he or she colors space #1 on the record sheet.

FS-591   Basic Word Skills (2-3)

Students may complete worksheets at their desks.

Finished work is placed in a manila folder near the kit. You can check the folder once a week!

Name _____

MY RECORD CARD

1 2 3 4 5 6 7 8
9 10 11 12 13 14
15 16 17 18 19 20

Name _____

MY RECORD CARD

1 2 3 4 5 6 7 9 10 11
13 14 16 8 19 20 21
12 24 15 17 18 31
23 25 27 28 30 32
22 35 26 29 33
34 36

FS-8301 Instant Idea Book

Using answer sheets

How to create a kit from activity cards:

- Put one set of activity cards in a box. (See Sample Card below.)

- Make an answer sheet for each set of cards. (See Answer Sheet below.)

- Duplicate enough answer sheets for everyone in your class. Staple or paste each student's answer sheet in a folder.

- The answer sheets will help students organize their work.

Sample Card

1. Shara and her brother Howard were going to do something they'd never done before — go on a whale watch.
   a. something new   b. catching whales   c. a brother and sister

2. Every winter the grey whales swim from Mexico to California. Boatloads of people go out to meet them.
   a. black whales   b. meeting seals   c. about the whales

3. Shara and Howard boarded a boat. They sailed off the coast of California. Suddenly they saw a huge grey rock near the boat. It was no rock, but a whale.
   a. on board   b. killer whales   c. big rocks

4. The whales seemed to enjoy the company. Some swam so close to the boat, the passengers were frightened. It was the most exciting day ever!
   a. falling overboard   b. meeting the whales   c. a boat trip

*What would you do if a whale was heading straight for your boat?

FS-3106 Getting the Main Idea

Copyright Frank Schaffer Publications, Inc.

FS-3106 Getting the Main Idea (4-5)

Answer sheets can be corrected quickly; make an answer key for each set of activity cards!

Using answer sheets

How to set up a kit for multiple-choice worksheets:

- Duplicate several copies of each worksheet.

- Laminate or paste worksheets on construction paper or tagboard.

- Put copies in a box.

- Duplicate enough answer sheets for each student.

sample worksheet

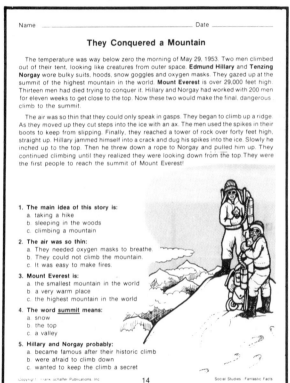

FS-550 Reading Comp.-Fantastic Facts (5-6)

Students write answers on answer sheet instead of actual worksheet.

Keep answer sheets at the front of the box, instead of in student desks.

answer sheet

Name _____ Date Started: _____
Date Done: _____

1. 1 _ 2 _ 3 _ 4 _ 5 _   11. 1 _ 2 _ 3 _ 4 _ 5 _
2. 1 _ 2 _ 3 _ 4 _ 5 _   12. 1 _ 2 _ 3 _ 4 _ 5 _
3. 1 _ 2 _ 3 _ 4 _ 5 _   13. 1 _ 2 _ 3 _ 4 _ 5 _
4. 1 _ 2 _ 3 _ 4 _ 5 _   14. 1 _ 2 _ 3 _ 4 _ 5 _
5. 1 _ 2 _ 3 _ 4 _ 5 _   15. 1 _ 2 _ 3 _ 4 _ 5 _
6. 1 _ 2 _ 3 _ 4 _ 5 _   16. 1 _ 2 _ 3 _ 4 _ 5 _
7. 1 _ 2 _ 3 _ 4 _ 5 _   17. 1 _ 2 _ 3 _ 4 _ 5 _
8. 1 _ 2 _ 3 _ 4 _ 5 _   18. 1 _ 2 _ 3 _ 4 _ 5 _
9. 1 _ 2 _ 3 _ 4 _ 5 _   19. 1 _ 2 _ 3 _ 4 _ 5 _
10. 1 _ 2 _ 3 _ 4 _ 5 _   20. 1 _ 2 _ 3 _ 4 _ 5 _

Slick tricks

Store posters on pants hangers in your closet. No more crumpled posters, maps or charts!

FS-721 Classroom Manners (K-3)

File materials by skill in manila folders. When you are ready to teach a particular skill, all your materials will be together!

Brighten file cabinets with posters!

Color code materials to indicate level of difficulty.

Example:
   Level 1 - red
   Level 2 - green
(Use press-on dots to indicate level or mount cards on colored construction paper.)

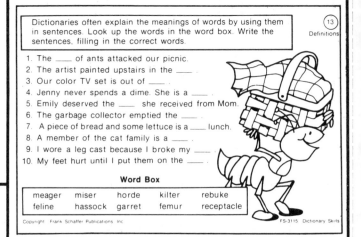

Dictionaries often explain the meanings of words by using them in sentences. Look up the words in the word box. Write the sentences, filling in the correct words.

⑬ Definitions

1. The ____ of ants attacked our picnic.
2. The artist painted upstairs in the ____.
3. Our color TV set is out of ____.
4. Jenny never spends a dime. She is a ____.
5. Emily deserved the ____ she received from Mom.
6. The garbage collector emptied the ____.
7. A piece of bread and some lettuce is a ____ lunch.
8. A member of the cat family is a ____.
9. I wore a leg cast because I broke my ____.
10. My feet hurt until I put them on the ____.

Word Box

| meager | miser | horde | kilter | rebuke |
| feline | hassock | garret | femur | receptacle |

Copyright Frank Schaffer Publications Inc.   FS-3115 Dictionary Skills

FS-3115 Dictionary Skills (2-3)

Students can progress from an easy level to a difficult level or, you can start more capable students at the higher level.

(multi-level kit)

Slick tricks

Store headsets in a five-gallon ice cream container — ends tangles!

Use a dressmaker's wheel* to make dotted lines on duplicating masters.

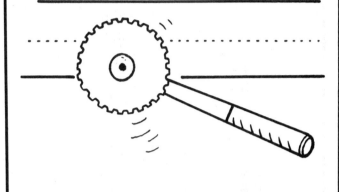

*Cost — about one dollar where sewing notions are sold.

Trace pictures by holding original and blank paper against window or place on lighted surface of overhead projector.

Cut cardboard into 9" x 12" rectangles to make clipboards. Attach clothespins to hold paper in place. Handy for students when they are away from their desks!

Slick tricks

Make no-cost, disposable easels from grocery store cartons.

Attach a pencil so students can write their names.

Pop extra copies of worksheets in a "homework box." Students can help themselves and use worksheets for fun.

Mix dry tempera paint with water and store in plastic liquid detergent bottles. Dispensing paint is easy — no mess!

Lids stuck on glue bottles? Remove lid (with nutcracker or pliers) and put vegetable oil* around bottle top **and** inside lid. Do this to new containers and they'll never stick!

*Petroleum jelly works too!

Slick tricks

Identify your pencils, pens and markers with a masking tape flag.

Keep track of students who used a particular worksheet by listing names on inside of worksheet folder.

Word
Skills · p.12

red group
yellow group · 12/1
green group 10/5

Cover five-gallon ice cream containers with colored paper. Students store construction paper or fabric scraps in containers according to color.

 Red
 Blue
 Green
Yellow

 Orange
 Black
Other Colors

?

 PURPLE

Store extra crayons in coffee cans sorted by color!

Learning activities

Self-Check Cards

File self-check cards in manila folders. When finished with the activity, student removes his or her answer sheet and puts self-check card under clothespin so it is ready to be used again.

class list

√ your name

clothespin

paper

file folder

How to use √ Self-Check √		
1. Place the self-check card on your paper.	2. Write your answers in the holes.	3. To check: turn the card over, place on your answers.

FS-822 Comprehension Skills (1-3)

Wipe-Away Cards

- Light-colored wax crayons erase better than black crayons.

- Use small carpet squares for erasing.

- Glue class list on back side of card. (Next year, glue new list on top.)

√ your name

FS-359 Comprehension Skills (2-3)

Gameboards

Glue 11″ x 16″ gameboards in a manila folder. Glue or write directions on front of folder. Put game cards in a plastic sandwich bag. Attach bag to folder with a clothespin.

Keep markers in a separate box or can.

☺ ☺ *indicates two players*

FS-8301 Instant Idea Book

Learning activities

Game Check-Out!

Allow students to check out a game and take it home for a few days. Students can play the game with parents, siblings or friends. Perfect for skill practice!

Game pieces should be sent home in a plastic bag.

Write each child's name on a 3″ x 5″ card. Keep cards together with a rubber band and store them in your desk drawer. When a student wants to check out a game, write the title of the game and date of return on the child's card.

Rain, Rain, Go Away

Gather a collection of "indoor recess" games for days when weather prohibits outdoor recess periods. Ask parents to donate games their children no longer use.

Helpful Tips

- Do not write skills on gameboards. Leave boards "blank" and use for any subject.

- Make games for two players — less waiting, more participation.

- Roll dice to decide who is first!

- Cut foam in cubes to make dice (quiet) — mark dots or numbers with felt-tip pen.

- Make games easy-to-store:

  - Glue inside manila folders.

  - Recycle old commerical gameboards (put your gameboard on top).

  - Buy inexpensive folding checkerboards (put your gameboard on top).

- Keep dice and markers separate from gameboards—makes gameboards easier to store!

- Make a spinner from a pencil and a paper clip.

- Color code materials to match storage area, i.e., purple dot on all reading games and purple dot on storage shelf.

Card holders:

(shoe box)

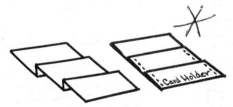

paper with stapled pockets

 **My ideas for using teaching materials . . .**

How to Save Time and Work

Time-management techniques for teachers:

Correcting Zone

help wanted

- Make a "To Do" list every morning. Check off tasks as they are completed. (See reproducible form on page 42.)

- Organize your work area.

- Set a time deadline for completing each task. Instead of spending a whole evening correcting papers, set a timer for a reasonable period of time and work as fast as you can. Stop when time is up — the rest of the evening is for you! You deserve it!

- Learn to say "No!"

- Identify the time wasters in your day — telephone? faculty lounge? Make the necessary changes to gain more time for yourself.

Please go over this at home

FS-8301 Instant Idea Book

Things I must do this week!

Monday

- [ ] #1 _____
- [ ] #2 _____
- [ ] #3 _____
_____
_____
_____

Tuesday

- [ ] #1 _____
- [ ] #2 _____
- [ ] #3 _____
_____
_____
_____

Wednesday

- [ ] #1 _____
- [ ] #2 _____
_____
_____
_____
_____

Thursday

- [ ] #1 _____
- [ ] #2 _____
_____
_____
_____
_____

Friday

- [ ] #1 _____
_____
_____
_____
_____
_____

FS-8301 Instant Idea Book

Free goodies to gather

Book Display (cardboard)

- from bookstores or card shops
  (available throughout the year)

Lunch Pail Display (cardboard)

- from variety stores
  (available during the fall)

Colorful, sturdy storage for your materials

Ask the store manager to save a display for you when you spot one you want!

Ask parents to save:	Use for:
carpet squares	sit-upons, desk top pads, wipe-away erasers
coffee (and other) cans with plastic lids	storage
computer cards	flash cards, bookmarks
computer paper	scratch paper, running off duplicating masters
five-gallon ice cream containers	storage
magazines, mail-order catalogs	cutting pictures
manila envelopes from the mail	sending papers or books home
old keys, caps from big felt-tip pens	game markers
shoe boxes	storage
socks	erasers for individual chalkboards
used books	classroom library
used games	rainy-day shelf
wallpaper sample books or scraps	art projects, folders, creative writing booklets
yarn	art projects, stitchery

FS-8301 Instant Idea Book

Checking student work

Finished Work Box

Train students to hand in papers right side up with their names at the top.
Label your work basket or box so students will place their papers correctly.

Use plastic dish pans for work boxes—they last forever!

Organize by Group

If you have several different groups of students, you may want each group to place papers in a different box.

Organize by Subject

Why not have a basket for each subject so papers are sorted for you?

Checking student work

Correcting Partners

Ask each student to choose a partner. When students exchange papers, the partners correct each other's work. You may want to re-assign partners every few months.

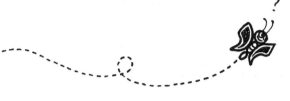

When a student is absent, his or her partner gathers work that the absent student is missing. That's one less thing for you to worry about!

A Positive Score

When you correct papers, mark the number of correct answers over the total number of questions. In other words, accentuate the positive! Write 8/10 instead of –2.

Double Grading

Give one grade for neatness and another grade for accuracy. When students know they are earning a separate grade for neatness, they will be motivated to work more carefully.

Checking student work

Alphabetized Class Roster

Write student names in your grade book in ABC order. Number the names, giving the first name number one. Add new students to the bottom of the list and number consecutively. Require students to write their names and numbers on their work. You, or a student, can quickly arrange papers in numerical order. The papers will be in ABC order as you correct them and record grades in your grade book.

Correcting Zone

Establish a Correcting Zone in your classroom. The zone can be a table, special area on the counter or windowsill, or several desks pushed together to make a table. Place red and blue pencils in a cup or basket on the table. Leave answer keys at the Correcting Zone. When students show you their completed work, give them permission to go to the Correcting Zone (without pencils or erasers). Red and blue pencils are used for correcting papers.

Checking student work

Bright Grades

Let the sun shine on all the right answers. Use a yellow highlighter, felt-tip marker or crayon. Highlight all correct answers as you grade papers. Highlight the most interesting sentence in stories written by your students.

Correcting Secretary

Select one student to be the "correcting secretary." Allow the secretary to sit at the teacher's desk with the answer key. Set a timer for 15 or 20 minutes. The correcting secretary checks completed work while the teacher circulates around the room, assisting students with the assignment. When the timer rings, let another student serve as correcting secretary. Check off names on a class list as students take turns so you can rotate the job.

Keep a chair next to your desk so students can wait quietly!

Checking student work

Easy Answer Columns

Insist that students make an answer column when doing math assignments from textbooks. Math papers can be corrected much faster when students list their answers. You can correct half a dozen papers at once by looking at several answer columns. My rule is that only the answer written in the answer column is the one that counts. If a student copies the right answer incorrectly in the column, it is still counted wrong. Learning to copy answers carefully is an important skill, especially for taking standardized tests.

To make the answer column, students can draw a line with a ruler or fold the paper.

answer column

Spread out a few papers and correct several at a time!

Touch Your Name

Before collecting papers, ask students to "touch your name." All the papers will have names written on them!

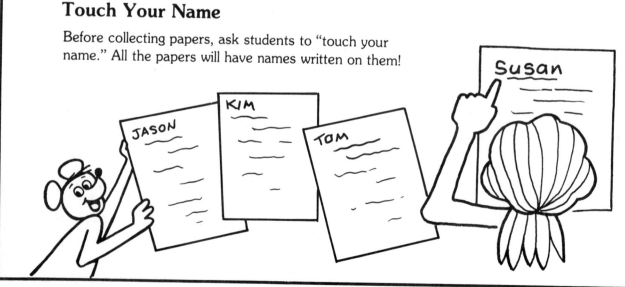

FS-8301 Instant Idea Book

Covering Answers

When students are going to correct their own math papers, tell them to color all answers with a yellow crayon first. Then call out or write correct answers on the chalkboard. Students will be unable to erase and change their answers.

This technique works well for reading worksheets and spelling tests too!

Touch Your Mistakes

Before collecting papers, tell students to find and fix punctuation and capitalization errors. For example: If students wrote three sentences, ask them to put their finger under the first letter of sentence number one. Ask if that letter is a capital. If not, students make it a capital. Then tell them to touch the punctuation mark at the end of sentence number one. Now look at sentence number two, etc.

> *Find and fix errors* **before** *I see your paper. Ready? Touch the capital letter at the beginning of sentence number one.*

Checking student work

Clipping Workbooks

When checking assignments from consumable workbooks, cut off the corners of pages that have been completed and corrected.

I use pinking shears for this since students can clip corners with scissors themselves!

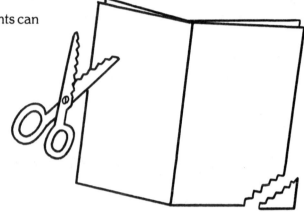

Sign Your Papers

When students swap papers for correcting, have the "corrector" sign his or her name at the bottom. Students are more careful when their names are on the corrected papers.

Special Colors

Use a color other than red for checking papers! Why not have a special color that is used **only** for perfect papers?

Examples: Miss Piggy Purple
14k Gold
Monster Green

Checking student work

Parent Helpers

Enlist clerical help from parents. Select tasks for parents to do at home on a weekly or bi-weekly basis. Each parent who signs up is responsible for the entire school year. You can give the parent a set of answer keys to keep at home. Their child takes home papers to be corrected and brings the corrected work back to school. You save time by merely checking work that has already been scored.

Welcome to open house!
Miss Sunshine   Room 6
Fourth Grade

Help Wanted

Sign up if you can do one job each week during the school year. Your child will bring papers home for correction.

Correct Instant Math Tests - Mondays and Thursdays - takes 20 minutes.

Check Read About Animals Kit: Fridays — takes about 45 minutes.

FS-8301 Instant Idea Book

Time-savers for students

Make sure each student keeps a shoe box in his or her desk. All small items must be stored in the box. This time-saver will help students quickly locate:

- scissors
- lunch money
- rulers
- pencils
- crayons, etc.

Designate one "spot" on the chalkboard where you write what students should do as soon as they enter the classroom in the morning or after recess. Your students will settle down quickly without wasting time!

Take out your ruler, pencils, scissors, and math book.

To help young children locate pages in basal readers, paper clip bookmarks in their books. Paper clip the pages of the story they read most recently. Students will automatically open their books to the next story. Simply move the marker as you go through the book.

84 85

Time-savers for teachers

Buy rubber stamps to save time rewriting the same message over and over! You can purchase custom-made rubber stamps at most stationary and photocopy stores.

Buy a red or green stamp pad so your messages will stand out!

Write frequently used directions on a chart instead of the chalkboard. When needed, hang the chart on the chalkboard. Saves time!

Spelling Sentences

1. Write a sentence for each spelling word.

2. **Underline** the spelling word in every sentence.

3. Make sure each sentence begins with a capital letter.

4. Is there a . ? or ! at the end of every sentence?

5. Touch your name!

True or False?

1. Write eight statements about the story you read. Make some statements true and some false.

2. Check your paper for:
   your name,
   capital letters and
   punctuation marks.

3. When finished, place your paper in the red basket.

See p. 34 for how to store charts.

Time-savers for teachers

If you write questions on the chalkboard to go with basal reader stories, social studies or science units, jot them down on a 5″ x 8″ index card as well. When the chalkboard is erased, you will have a record of the questions. You can re-use them when you teach those units again. Make sure you write down the name of the unit or page numbers of the basal reader story.

Be prepared!

At the beginning of the school year, make kits for substitute teachers. Duplicate "blank plans" for a substitute. When you write your plans, just fill in the form.

Staple blank substitute plans on the front of a construction paper folder. Make six folders. Duplicate and put inside each folder:

- reading comprehension worksheet

- class list

- math drill sheet

- following directions worksheet

- directions for easy art activity

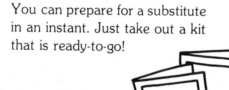

You can prepare for a substitute in an instant. Just take out a kit that is ready-to-go!

Substitute Plans ★Team captain of each group is a dependable student.

Date _____

8:30 Opening, Lunch Count
8:45 Reading
      Group A _____
(Fri. SEA Kit   B _____
on hall cart.)
      C _____
9:45   Recess (Duty _____)
10:00 Spelling (test on Friday)
10:15 Language Arts
11:00 M, W, F-PE; T, Th-Music
11:30 Story Time
11:45 Lunch (Duty _____)
12:30 Math
1:30   Recess (Duty _____)
2:00   Soc. St./Sci. Art(W)
3:00   Current Events:
3:10   Dismissal
Notes:
? Ask Miss Sunshine—Room 21

Tell another teacher about your "basic battle plan." Refer the sub to this person for help.

Time-savers for teachers

Speed up lesson plan writing!

1. On a strip of tagboard, list your daily time schedule. Clip the tagboard to the left side of your plan book instead of rewriting the same information every week.

8:30	Opening
8:45-9:45	Reading
9:50-10:00	Recess
10:00-10:50	Language
(Spelling test on Fridays)	
11:00-11:50	Math
12:00-12:40	Lunch
12:45-1:00	Story
1:00-1:50	Social Studies
1:50	Recess
2:00-3:00	Science
Library— Thursday 2:30-3:00	

2. Open a manila folder and list days of the school week vertically; subjects and time schedule horizontally. Cut windows and paper clip folder on top of plan book. Write lesson plans through the window holes. Move the file folder each week!

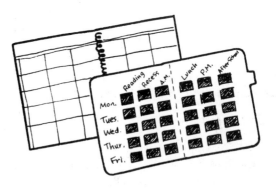

3. Draw lines on two blank duplicating masters to make one look like the right-hand and one like the left-hand page of your plan book. Then jot down weekly subjects and time schedule for your class. Duplicate or photocopy 36 copies of each, punch with a three-hole punch and put in a binder. Use this instead of your plan book. The subjects and time schedule are already there. You just fill in the details.

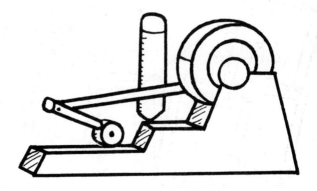

Time-savers for teachers

Mark handwriting guidelines on the chalkboard with a permanent black felt pen.

Makes writing on the chalkboard simple!

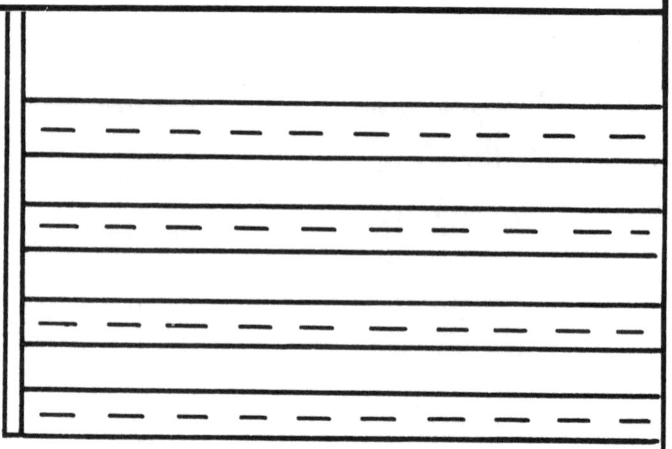

Set up and duplicate forms for notes you write frequently.

_____ has permission to call home.

Mrs. Gruber

on _____
        date

_____ has permission to go to the school library.

Mrs. Gruber

on _____
        date

TO: School Nurse
FROM: _Mrs. Gruber_

_____ is not feeling well.

Date: _____

TO: Film Crew
FROM: _Mrs. Gruber_

Please bring a film projector to my room no later than _____

on _____ .

Use the reproducible notes on page 57. Sign your name before duplicating!

To: _____

From: _____

On: _____

_____

_____

_____

_____

Just a Reminder:

Please send to school tomorrow:

_____

_____

_____

_____

Thank you,

_____

_____

To: _____ From: _____ On: _____

_____

_____

_____

_____

_____

_____

Time-savers for teachers

Make a class list on a duplicating master so you don't have to copy names by hand. To save paper, you can put several copies of your class list on a master, duplicate and cut into strips.

At the beginning of the school year, have each student write his or her phone number on three class lists. Keep one list of phone numbers at home, one in the office and staple the extra list inside your grade book.

Laminate a name tag on each student's desk with clear contact paper. It lasts all year! Ideas:

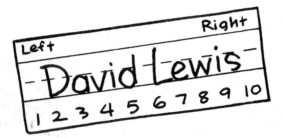

See reproducible name tags on page 59.

If your classroom is far away from the office or lounge, keep a supply box "hidden" somewhere.

Supply Box:
- extra duplicating masters
- pens and pencils
- scissors
- class list

I keep mine in my office mailbox.

FS-8301 Instant Idea Book

Set aside 10 minutes at the end of each week for a class cleanup. Write jobs for each student on index cards. After the cleanup, collect the cards, shuffle and redistribute next week.

Idea!

Play a record during the class cleanup. Tell students they may talk but you must be able to hear the music.

It's amazing! The record keeps the noise level down!

Job Suggestions:

- sharpen pencils
- tidy classroom library
- clean sink
- tidy art center
- clean chalk ledges
- clap erasers
- dust
- return books to library
- clean desk tops row #1
- clean desk tops row #2
- clean desk tops row #3
- clean desk tops row #4
- clean desk tops row #5
- water plants
- empty trash

Don't lose a minute

Recording absences and counting "lunch buyers" can waste valuable time. Here are some useful, time-saving ideas!

1. Check-In Board

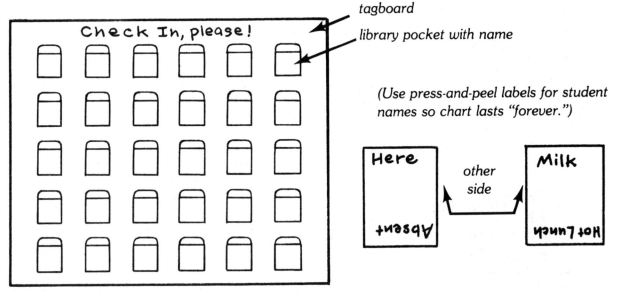

tagboard

library pocket with name

(Use press-and-peel labels for student names so chart lasts "forever.")

Here

Absent

other side

Milk

Hot Lunch

At the end of each day, turn all cards back to Absent.

2. Write each student's name on a clothespin and clip pins around the edge of a coffee can. Students drop their pins in the can when they enter the classroom. Remaining pins show names of absentees. Ask a student helper to clip the clothespins back onto the can at the end of each day.

Check in, please!

 **My ideas for saving time & work**

FS-8301 Instant Idea Book